Sleepy Socks
& Sometime Rhymes

Teena Raffa-Mulligan

Poems for Home & Classroom

SEA SONG PUBLICATIONS | AUSTRALIA

Copyright © 2019 by Teena Raffa-Mulligan

All rights reserved. No part of this publication may be reproduced, distributed or transmitted in any form or by any means, without prior written permission.

Sea Song Publications
Warnbro
Western Australia 6169
Email: sea-song@bigpond.com

Cover Design: Veronica Rooke
Sleepy Socks & Sometime Rhymes/ Teena Raffa-Mulligan. -- 1st ed.
ISBN 978-0-6482503-8-8
Book Layout © 2019 BookDesignTemplates.com

Previously published in *The School Magazine*: The Boss of Me, The Sub's Complaint, New Shoes for Sam, Hide and Seek, Leaf Lace, Umbrella Tree, Peacock Patrol, Sea Speak, Pirates in the Den, Book World, Storyteller, No Everyday Chair, Grandma and the Alien, Way Out Week, The Visitor, Grandpa Goes to Mars, I Can, Moving Marvel, The Party of the Year.

Published in *Contagious*: Grandpa Goes to Mars, Grandma and the Alien
Published in *One Minute till Bedtime*: No Peas
Published in *Let's Jabberwocky*: The Sub's Complaint
Published in *The New School Paper*: The Call of the Wind, Way Out Week
Published in *Quark*: The Sub's Complaint.
Published in *Celebrate End of Year Reciter*: Santa's New Clothes

Image credits: Children playing - Image courtesy of Vlado at FreeDigitalPhotos.net; Children doing yoga - Image courtesy of sattva at FreeDigitalPhotos.net; Aliens - Image courtesy of Simon Howden at FreeDigitalPhotos.net; Countryside kids - Image courtesy of Stuart Miles at FreeDigitalPhotos.net; Fairy tales -Image courtesy of AKARAKINGDOMS at FreeDigitalPhotos.net

Contents

Me 1
Moving Marvel
I Can
Sole Mates

My world 5
Sleepy Socks
The Boss of Me
Mad Dad for Sale
Eek! It's Zeke!
Yawn
The Sub's Complaint
Hide and Seek
New Shoes for Sam
Jumping Jack
Dinner with a Dinosaur
Something is Under the Bed
Eggs-asperated
No Peas
Fruit Salad
Breakfast at Rosie's
The Party of the Year

Our world 35
Leaf Lace
Umbrella Tree
Peacock Patrol

Rottnest Island Visitors
Sea Speak
Sea
A Day at the Beach
Windy...
Storm Safe
Fragments
The Call of the Wind

Other worlds...53
Grandma and the Alien
Way Out Week
The Visitor
It
Grandpa Goes to Mars

Story worlds..67
Pirates in the Den
No Everyday Chair
The Everywhere Chair
Prince
Storyteller
Book World
Daffodil
Knit Knack
A Mouse in the House
Sir Quackalot Saves the Day
Santa's New Clothes

Me

Moving marvel

I can
Banana bend
Licorice twist
Jelly wibble wobble.

See me
Caterpillar creep
Snake slither
Deer dash and dart.

I am
Rock steady
Tree tall
River rush and flow.

Love this
Body mine
Body strong
This moving marvel.

I can

I can turn cartwheels,
I can do splits,
Handstands and headstands,
back and front flips.

I can do rollovers,
round like a ball,
and stand on my hands
with my feet on the wall.

I can do star jumps
and reach for the sky,
and run so fast
you'd think I could fly.

But I can't catch the wind
as it flees down the hill,
or stop Father Time
and make him stand still.

Sole mates

My feet are great, they're just first-rate,
each one a match with its sole mate.
One left, one right, to take me places,
dance and jump and run fast races.

I've ten fine toes that like to twitch,
And they can reach to scratch knee itch.
When I stand tall on tippy toe—
Don't need to wait until I grow.

The cake tin is within my reach
And then I scarper to the beach
To leap the waves that lap the shore.
I kick, sand-flick then race some more.

If every car and bus broke down
It wouldn't stop me getting round,
For I'd still get from here to there,
My feet would take me everywhere.

My World

Sleepy socks

My socks start out the way they should.
Toes snugged, heels hugged, all looking good.
But as the day tick-tocks away,
I find my socks just do not stay.
Bit by bit they slowly sneak
Down low until my ankles peek,
Then with another slippery slide,
Way down in my shoes they hide.
"Your socks have gone to sleep," says Mum.
"We'll wake them now. Up they come."
Toes snugged, heels hugged, all looking good
My socks are sitting as they should,
But only for a while and then
They start their slippery slide again.

The boss of me

When I'm taller than Mum and stronger than Dad
and folks call me 'mister' instead of 'young lad',
I'll never eat broccoli, cabbage or beans,
and whenever I like I'll sleep in my jeans.
I'll scream, shout and holler and act like a clown
and no one will tell me to keep the noise down.
I'll not use a timer when having my showers,
but run the hot water for hours and hours.
I'll not bother with soap and shampoo and stuff.
If I'm a bit smelly, well so what? That's tough.
I'll sleep until midday and breakfast on cake.
If there's crumbs on my quilt, I'll just give it a shake.
I won't share my chocolate, I'll eat the whole lot.
If I'm called a meanie, I won't care a jot.
When I'm older and bigger, no longer a kid,
no one will boss me around like they did.
Only I will decide what I can and can't do.
I'll be boss of myself. You heard: me – that's who.

Mad dad for sale

My dad's always getting mad,
his temper's really, really bad.
He said to stay here in my room,
he made me miss the best cartoon.

If I were a giant instead of me
and he made me really angry
I would kick him to the stars
and perhaps he'd land on Mars.

Or I'd lock him in the zoo.
Yes, that's just the thing to do,
he could growl and pace about
and I'd never let him out.

But I'm not a giant at all,
I am me and only small.
What can I do about a dad
who is always getting mad?

When we didn't want our van,
our dad sold it to a man.

Perhaps that's the thing to do
with a dad you don't want, too.

I'm sure some folks would find
he was what they had in mind.
I'd wrap them Dad to take away
and I'd shout, "Hip, hip hooray!"

But could I wave goodbye,
or would I start to cry?
For perhaps without my dad
I would feel a little sad.

Who would let me dive from him
when he took me for a swim?
Help me hunt the big white shark
in our garden after dark?

Who would wrestle, run and play,
help me laugh the day away?
Or talk away my fears
and gently dry my tears?

And my dad does not sell me
though I often get quite angry
so I guess it's not so bad
to have a dad who's sometimes mad.

Eek! It's Zeke!

"Look out!" kids shriek.
"It's Zeke the freak!"
They run away,
Won't let me play.

They cringe in fear
If I come near,
Afraid of germs
And nits and worms.

They say I'm crazy
Mean and lazy;
Too loud, too rough,
Always acts tough.

It makes me sad
They treat me bad.
I wish they knew
I want friends too.

Yawn

Yawn a little, yawn a lot

tie your pigtails in a knot.

Squiggle, squirm and scuff your toes,

clear your throat and blow your nose.

Let Teacher know you've had enough

of learning all this clever stuff.

Much more fun to yell and shriek.

Why wait till Friday? End this week!

The sub's complaint

Player:
Me sideline sitting?
Again? I'm quitting!
It's not my turn,
just check your sheet
I didn't get to play
at all last week!
There! You see,
the sub was me,
that means today
I ought to play.

Coach:
You know this game we've got to win.
I can't afford to leave you in,
for that would mean that Sue was out,
and she's best shot, without a doubt.

Player:
I know, coach, but just the same,
does one player lose a game?

Coach:
It's not because you drop the ball,
I know you never mean to fall.

Player:
Well, sitting won't improve my game,
for watching isn't quite the same.
If I'm to get a chance to learn
you have to let me take my turn.
It isn't fair to play the best
all the time and not the rest.

You always say that we're a team.
These days it doesn't really seem
very much to me like one.
For how can I have any fun
just watching all the others play
day after dreary, dreary day?

It only makes me rather glum.
I sit and wonder why I've come.
Be a sport, coach, hey fair go!
Winning isn't all, you know.

Hide and seek

One – Run!

The count's on.

Two, three –

Follow me.

Go! Go!

Don't be slow.

Quick! Race!

Find a place.

Four, five –

In we dive

Curl small

Like a ball

Six – Shush!

And don't push.

Se-ven –

Eight, nine, ten –

Let's see

Where they'll be.

Here? There?

Wonder where.

No, please,

Don't you sneeze!

Uh oh!

Now she'll know.

Ah ha!

There you are!

Peek a – boo!

Nan found you!

New shoes for Sam

Sam needs new shoes.
What will he choose?
Mum says, "We'll see,
Just come with me."

In the street
So many feet,
Limping, lurching,
Marching past,
Strolling, striding,
Running fast.

Shoes for work
And shoes for play,
For summer sun
And winter day.

Tippety tap toes
And clickety clack heels,
Spinning, turning
Roller wheels.

Slippers slop-slapping,
Flippers flop-flapping,
Faster and fleeter
Or totter and teeter.

Inside the store
Are shoes galore.
They sure confuse –
What will Sam choose?
Mum says, "We'll try
Before we buy."

Shoes off, shoes on,
This, then that one.
Too big, too small,
Not right at all.

Slip sliders,
High riders,
Heel crunchers,
toe bunchers.

All wrong,
So-o-o long,
Bub cries,
Mum sighs...
Sam grins
And spins.
Oh yeah,
This pair!

No squash or squeeze,
Mum nods, "Yes please."
Sam has new shoes
He got to choose.

Jumping Jack

Mum's boy Jack is a dynamo,
Always moving, on the go.
Day in, day out he leaps about,
He's Jumping Jack without a doubt.

Jack's mum cries, "Won't you be still?"
And Jack replies, "I will, I will!"
But soon his toe begins to twitch,
He has to scratch an awful itch.

Grandma says it must be worms,
They dose him up but still he squirms.
Grandpa thinks it is the treats,
"He's too allergic, no more sweets!"

But still Jack jiggles and wriggles about
Every time they take him out.
It drives his mother to despair,
She begs, "Jack, sit still in your chair."

They try all sorts of pills and potions,
Herb concoctions, soothing lotions.

Nothing works, he's still the same.
That's why Jumping Jack's his name.

Then Dad's mate Blue knows what to do
Because he's had that problem too
With his kelpie Mad Dog Mick
Before he found what did the trick.

Mick had driven Bluey crazy—
Now he was just doggone lazy.
"We'll try it out," Dad says to Blue,
"We've no idea what else to do."

Next day Jack wakes before the sun.
Mum is waiting, dressed to run.
While the others are still sleeping,
Out they go so quietly creeping.

Mum drives to the greyhound track
and chases her boy up and back
Jack is speedy, lightning fast.
Mum lags behind, always last.

Still she urges young Jack on
Till all his energy is gone.

When she takes him out that day
Not once does Jack's mum have to say,
"For goodness sakes, sit still, will you,"
Because he sleeps the whole day through.

He misses lunch at Auntie Jill's,
Grocery shopping and paying bills,
Dozes while Mum buys some clothes,
A potted rose and a garden hose.

He doesn't wake till day is done
Then up he leaps to have some fun.
 Mum looks at Dad and says, "Oh dear,
Our Jumping Jack is back, I fear."

Dinner with a dinosaur

I went out for a walk one day
all by myself far, far away.
Susie begged, "Please take me too,"
but I said, "No I won't take you.

"Your legs won't walk as far as mine
and I'll be gone a long, long time.
While I am gone, you have your nap
and I will bring you something back."

I packed myself some milk and cheese,
some tissues should I need to sneeze,
a piece of cake and lots of dates
and then we went to our front gates.

"Bye," said Mum, "and don't forget this."
She bent right down and gave me a kiss.
I wiped it off for it was wet,
hugged small Sue, then off I set.

For a while I walked and sang a song.
I marched, I strode, I strolled along

Past houses, trees and people too.
Sometimes I said, "How do you do?"

At last I thought I ought to run.
I raced with myself and always won.
Running fast with the wind in my hair
it wasn't long before I was there.

I settled myself upon a small hill.
It was awfully quiet and all was still.
I took out my cake, my dates and my cheese.
Then a voice said, "Can I have some, please?"

I looked all around but no one was there.
"You're mean," it said, "why won't you share?"
"Where are you?" I asked, for I couldn't see.
"Silly!" it said. "You're sitting on me!"

Then the hill moved and I fell right off.
It shuddered, shook and gave a loud cough.
"My goodness!" I said. "Oh gosh! Oh golly!"
For what do you think that I could see?

It looked to me like a dinosaur

but I rubbed my eyes as I wasn't sure.
Whatever it was, it was gigantic.
My legs were shaking and I felt frantic.

But just when I started to run away, it said,
"Don't go," and asked me to stay.
We sat there together and nibbled cheese.
I offered it cake. It said, "Yes, please."

Then we played games, I slid down its neck,
and what a long slide that was, by heck.
I sat on its nose with my toes on its chin.
"That tickles," it said and started to grin.

When I said, "Goodbye, I really must go,"
"Come again," it invited, but I don't know.
Still I ran and chuckled at what I'd seen
for no one I knew had been where I'd been

and no one I knew – of that I was sure –
had ever had dinner with a dinosaur.
When I got home I told my mum.
She said, "That's nice, next time we'll come."

Something is under the bed

It was night and the light in the passage was on,
The children tucked in and the visitors gone
When the house was aroused by an ear-splitting yell.
"Something is under my bed!" yelled Nell.
Silence broken, all woken, what had Nell said?
She really thought something was under her bed?
"It's true, I tell you, I am not telling lies!
It's moaning and groaning, you must hear its sighs.
Its bumping and thumping has got me so scared
And I would sneak a peek if only I dared.
I do know it must go. Please come get it out!
It's thumping and bumping my bed all about
And it's started to fart with a terrible pong."
A crash caused a dash to see what was wrong.

Nell's father and mother, sister and brother
Were in such a rush they tripped over each other.
They gasped when it passed with a horrible roar,

Crawled the wall, had a fall in its flight to the door.
Wrecked it to exit, then was gone in a blink
Leaving behind it the most terrible stink.

Mum rubbed her eyes and said, "What was that?
A bear with long hair and a tail like a cat?"
Dad frowned. "No, a hound with a horn on its head.
That's what was hiding under Nell's bed."
"Not at all," said small Paul, "it had shiny smooth skin
And no horn, I'd have sworn, but a beard on its chin."
"Well yes," agreed Tess, "it did have a beard,
But scales and twin tails that looked rather weird."
They weren't sure what they saw, disagreed what they'd seen;
What the something from under Nell's bed might have been.
Nell said, "I don't care what it was or could be
As long as it's not in my bedroom with me."

Eggs-asperated

Eggs for breakfast, dinner, brunch;

In salad sandwiches for lunch.

Eggs every night for dinner too.

I ask you, what's a kid to do?

Eggs with sausages and peas,

In tuna pasta bake with cheese.

Scrambled, poached and curried,

Plain hard boiled when mealtime's hurried.

My Nan could win Olympic gold

For eggs-elence since she was told

I liked eggs best. My BIG mistake.

I should have chosen chocolate cake.

No peas

Oh please,
no peas,
no peas today.
I must
try just
a few you say?
No Aunt,
you can't
make me eat peas.
An egg
I'll beg;
let me choose cheese.
I'd eat
peas sweet
and crunchy raw.
Not these
hot peas
and that's for sure.
I'd spew
and you
would hate the smell.
I guess

the mess
would irk as well.
I can't –
I shan't
eat peas. No way.
I won't.
I don't
care what you say.
My lips
are zipped –
they're shut quite tight,
No peas
will pass
through them tonight.
I sniff
a whiff
of something good...
A treat
so sweet:
Choc slice for pud.
I find
my mind
I've changed on peas.
Last one!
All gone!
Dessert? Yes, please!

Fruit salad

Reached peach, sweet and juicy,
drips and dribbles down my chin.
Plump plum, round and rosy,
fresh flesh, satin skin.

Dappled apple, crisp and tasty,
crunch, munch, eat a chunk.
Shared pear, over ripe,
slushy, mushy. Yuk! What gunk.

Draped grapes, green and purple,
slurp, burp, spit the pips.
Berries, cherries, apricots,
chipped, whipped, served in dips.

Beaut fruit, sweet treat,
eat it each and every day
sliced, diced, choose juiced,
or have it any other way.

Breakfast at Rosie's

Breakfast at Rosie's
at half past eight.
Muffins at Rosie's,
warm on the plate.
Join us at Rosie's,
please don't be late
for breakfast at Rosie's,
it'll be great.
We're all here at Rosie's,
don't make us wait.
Hurry to Rosie's,
slip through the gate.
You'll get to Rosie's
fast if you skate,
whizzing to Rosie's
at such a rate.
Rush into Rosie's –
what's today's date?
Surprise at Rosie's –
"Happy birthday, Kate!"

The party of the year

Contrary Mary from Down's Dairy
got to be the Christmas fairy.
I heard Tom tossed her and her wand
right into the goldfish pond.

And silly Sally from the deli
ate so much red raspberry jelly,
chocolate, turkey, cake, ice cream,
I'm not surprised she burst a seam.

Skinny Minnie tore her pinny,
stuck the donkey's tail on Timmy.
Poor old cat shrieked something shocking,
tried to climb Aunt Martha's stocking.

Uncle Terry came by ferry,
drank the punch and was so merry,
danced a jig without his clothes –
shocked Aunt Martha, I suppose.

Then Wanda's Rhonda from down yonder
took a ride on Harry's Honda,
ended up in Cooper's Creek,
cried as if she'd sprung a leak.

And Jace the Ace won all the races
till John tied his sneaker laces.
All the goings on at that party
were certainly a sight to see.

Yes, everyone had fun but me
'cos all I saw was our TV,
and all I got was chicken pox -
lots and lots and lots of spots.

Our World

Leaf lace

Lace maker
Toils secretly
Tucked out of sight;
Creates ornate
Patterns
Until they're just right.
Delicate, intricate
Handiwork done,
Designer departs
To start
The next one.
Serrates, decorates
All my plants in this way.
I confess
I'm impressed
At this leaf lace display.

Umbrella tree

Umbrella tree

shelter me

beneath your leafy canopy.

Let rain fall;

wild wind squall;

it won't bother me at all.

Your branches spread;

shield my head;

I think a thank you should be said.

Peacock patrol

Courtyard guard
dressed to impress
in his distinctive uniform;
such finery so proudly worn.

Collar blue
of varied hue,
dappled jacket, coat tails grand,
spectacular when fully fanned.

Crow's sleek coat
of satin sheen,
though smart, cannot compare
with the guardsman's finer wear.

Head held high,
with watchful eye,
he surveys the sheltered scene,
leaf-strewn carpet, verdant green.

With lordly strut,
inspects the steps.
He takes his duty seriously
and behaves imperiously.

His noisy neighbour's
raucous cry
does not disturb his regal stroll,
this splendid bird on ground patrol.

Rottnest Island visitors

Bare feet,
dusky, dusty.
Silent footfalls
slip with ease
through trees
that shelter, shade;
keep time to
breeze breath,
wave song.
This land. His land.

Shod feet,
encased, tight-laced,
pound path
through trees
that shelter, shade;
keep time to
fast-paced tempo
of time's race.
Island. My land.

Same sun, same sky;
same shimmering sea
sweeps pristine shore.
Same sentinel trees
still guard this ocean gem.
His land. My land.
Our land. Island.

Sea speak

Wave whisper, shore song,
so sweet lullaby.
Hush awhile – listen!
You'll hear if you try.

Wind wail and sea shriek,
rage, rumble and roar.
Storm's angry voice
no one can ignore.

Whatever its mood –
shout, murmur or sigh –
when sea speaks to me
it asks no reply.

I listen, I hear
and I understand
the special language
of sea, sky and sand.

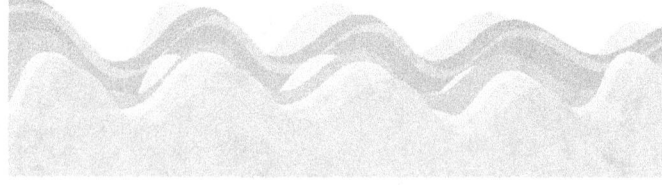

Sea

Who walked these shores
and sat upon these rocks
that thrust their fists
into the churning waves
that crash and thunder like a storm
or gently lap like tongue on ice cream cone?
Who felt this breeze
that strokes my cheek
and lifts my hair,
that says so softly it is there?
Who heard the gulls
that wheel and shriek
against the backdrop of sky canvas
in clean sweeps of Nature's brush?
I do not know.
Yet I am sure the question was the same.
Unspoken – yet echoed
through Time's turning leaves: Why are we
here?

A day at the beach

The sea rushed up to say hello
and kissed me on my tippy toe.
I chased the breeze along the shore,
it snatched the brand new hat I wore
and skimmed it off across the sand,
it lost its yellow daisy band.

I squealed out loud and off I ran,
then we played 'catch it if you can'.
Each time I reached for it, that breeze
plucked it away, oh what a tease.
It tossed it on the waves to float,
a funny-looking bobbing boat.

A cheeky gull perched on its brim.
Nana laughed. "Good luck to him."
She said we'd buy another hat,
no need to cry, so that was that.

Now here I lean on window sill,
rugged up against the winter chill,
drinking chocolate hot and sweet,

snuggly slippers on my feet,
watching lightning slash the sky.
I jump at thunder's loud reply.

The rain makes rivers in the yard;
the wind slams doors and windows hard.
I close my eyes, remembering that
Nan bought me such a pretty hat
to shade my face from summer sun,
then took me to the beach to run.

I didn't have that hat for long
because the breeze was very strong.
It stole it from me in a blink.
That made me sad. I didn't think
I'd giggle at the memory
of summer day down by the sea.

Windy...

On Monday the wind simply wanted to play.
It teased my balloon, made it dance a ballet.
It chased me and my ball all round the park.
Nan tried to keep up. She said, "What a lark!"

On Tuesday the wind stole my favourite cap.
It wanted my scarf but it didn't get that.
So it pulled my hair and pushed me hard
and kicked up the leaves in our front yard.

Wednesday's wind was unfriendly and chill.
When we went walking up the hill
it slapped my cheeks and nipped my nose,
poked icy fingers through my clothes.

Dad kept Bub snug inside his vest,
that frosty wind it never guessed
as it hurried us home with mournful moan
and swept through the trees with an awful groan.

We locked it outside and ignored how it cried,

so all through Thursday it wailed and sighed.
It whined at the windows, rattled the door knob
and moaned round the house with a miserable sob.

On Friday the wind grew fierce and wild
and ripped up our fence like an angry child;
went on a rampage, wrecked houses and sheds,
and me and Bub shook with fear in our beds.

By Saturday morning its anger had passed.
Its bluster had gone, it was quiet at last.
Everyone helped from morning till night
to clear up the mess and set things right.

We all celebrated a job well done,
had treats to eat and lots of fun.

On Sunday the wind whispered soft in my ear
In a voice so low only I could hear,
"I'll catch my breath and rest today,
but I'll be back again to play."

Storm safe

Let clouds muster,

Winds bluster,

Rain pound,

Thunder sound

Like cymbal clash.

Let lightning slash,

Scissor inky sky.

I will not cry.

I'm all right

Through blackest night,

Tight-ball curled

In my own world.

Rug-huddled,

Snug-bundled

Till storm's past,

Calm at last.

1.

Butterfly

flutters by,

paper fragment

on errant breeze.

2.

Dry branches

twist and tangle

in sky puzzle

without solution.

The call of the wind

The wind whispered softly through grass and
through gum.
She heard it call clearly, invitingly, "Come!"
Felt fingers of freshness caressing her face,
ruffling her fur with such gentle embrace.

The earth had a freshness that comes after rain
and she heard the wind calling, again and again:
"Come and run with me, seek freedom, take
flight!"
Its call roused a longing to know such delight.
It whispered so softly, in murmur so low.
It beckoned her, "Come," and she wanted to go.

To forage in green grass new-kissed by the rain,
to taste of its sweetness and know once again
how it feels to run freely with life unrestrained,
to run with the wind, by a fence uncontained.

She pricked up her ears, her body was tense.
Her heart filled with longing, she leaped at the
fence.

The sweet taste of freedom was brief –
incomplete –
for she soon heard the sound of hurrying feet.

Familiar voice calling, she paused in her flight.
Gentle voice saying, "I know it's not right.
I'm sorry, my girl, but I can't let you go,
for the ranger might catch you and you'd no more know
even brief tastes of freedom – a short walk each day.
It's no compensation – what more can I say?"

Confined by four walls, she restlessly paced.
the wind's call to freedom would not be erased.
She heard it still calling, no longer so low.
Her heart ached with longing, with wanting to go.
She yearned for its freedom, she longed so to run,
for it was its own master, it answered to none.

Now it rapped on the windows, crept under the door
and its taunting call mocked like a thorn in the paw
as she lay down to sleep on a cold concrete floor.

Other Worlds

Grandma and the alien

The alien was sitting
behind Grandma's chair.
She kept on knitting,
unaware it was there.

It sneezed
and she wheezed,
and said, "I declare!
A breeze if you please
just ruffled my hair."

The alien came close
and crouched by Gran's knee.
She wrinkled her nose.
What could that smell be?

It neared
and she peered,
and said, "Goodness me!
What's that
on the mat?
I just can't quite see."

The alien reposed,
curled up by Gran's side.
She nodded, then dozed.
Oh my, she felt tired.

It darted –
she started –
her eyes opened wide.
She knit one,
then slipped one,
and said, "Go outside!"

The alien sighed,
and Gran murmured low
as she measured a side –
an inch left to go.

It mumbled,
she grumbled,
and said, "I don't know
why a cat
doesn't scat
when you tell it to go."

The alien stared
deep into Gran's eyes.
She no longer cared
if her work was to size.
It muttered,
she uttered
a squeal of surprise
as she whirled
and she twirled
and then started to rise.

The alien chanted a mystical word.
The room slipped
and slanted,
the fan faster whirred.
Gran wailed,
but she sailed
through the window unheard.

She listed
and twisted,
quite startled a bird.
Gran soon was spinning
at top speed through space.
Would have been winning
it if was a race.

Passed stars
and red Mars
at a frightening pace,
all because of the force
in an alien's face.

The alien was sitting
right in grandma's chair,
doing her knitting
with particular care,
a smile
all the while
on its countenance rare.
It knit one
and slipped one,
then murmured, "So there!"

Way out week

On Monday a Martian played Monopoly with me.
On Tuesday a tourist from Taurus had tea.
On Wednesday I went where the weather was warm,
vacationed on Venus, avoided Earth's storm.
On Thursday I thought I'd throw three or four
meteorites moonwards – or maybe more.
On Friday I fried fish on flaming fireballs,
went walking on one of Woomera's west walls.
Saturday I saw satellites, spaceships and stars,
made marvellous missions between Moon and Mars.
On Sunday I sent to Saturn for supper:
crispy crustaceans, crab crepes and a cuppa.
My week was so wonderful, weird and way out
this next will seem boring, of that I've no doubt.

The visitor

I touched down from Pluto at a quarter to three.
Just called for a visit and afternoon tea.
I'd heard that the scones with jam and fresh cream
were simply delicious, a taste treat supreme.
But no sooner did I step through my ship door
than the welcoming crowd gave out a great roar.
"A monster!" they howled as if with one voice,
and I shuddered to hear such a terrible noise,
and choked on the dust they raised as they ran
till no one was left there, not even one man.
I looked around, but I couldn't see
a monster at all – they must have meant me.
I sighed as I turned and went back to my ship.
I'd expected to have such a very nice trip.
I switched on the gizmo, set my course by the stars:
perhaps my reception would be better on Mars.

It

It munched them
and crunched them,
declared them delicious:
a fountain,
a mountain,
a bridge
and three fishes.

It slurped, then
it burped and
announced the meal sufficient;
shook its heads
about the beds –
pronounced them deficient.

It then chose
a short doze
on the balmy blue Pacific,
blinked its eye,
waved goodbye,
and went somewhere unspecific.

Grandpa goes to Mars

In November 2023
when Grandpa Green turned eighty three,
he said one day he rather thought
he'd like to be an astronaut.

"If I wait another year
there's a chance I'll not be here,"
he said to Gran at morning tea.
She nodded wisely, "Yes, I see.
You really can't afford to wait,
tomorrow it might be too late."

She helped him polish pate and boots,
packed gumleaf tea, alfalfa shoots,
carrot juice and pumpkin seeds,
assorted plants that some called weeds;
combed his beard, brushed his hat,
pressed clean trousers while he sat
planning out his strategy
of where to go and who to see.

At last he sighed contentedly,

flexed his fingers and trick knee,
announced he'd travel first by train
to Sydney, where he'd take a plane
to New York, then to NASA's base,
Miami, where he'd put his case
to join the programme's training scheme
and be a member of the team
preparing for a trip to Mars,
and on towards the nearest stars.

Soon Grandpa straightened up his tie,
picked up his bag and said goodbye,
gave Gran's wrinkled cheek a peck,
instructed, "Bank my pension cheque;
don't forget to feed the chooks,
plant more carrots, keep the books."
He set off down the rocky track
with cheery call, "I'll soon be back."

But arriving at his destination,
Grandpa caused a mild sensation,
announcing that he'd come to be
an astronaut at eighty-three.
The secretary suppressed a grin
as he ushered Grandpa in
to see Commander Hank Jardine

and his small selection team.
They heard what Grandpa had in mind,
hid muffled laughter well behind
quickly raised official files,
snuffles, snorts and slipping smiles.

Jardine took himself in hand,
cleared his throat, "I understand
that travelling in a rocket ship
could seem a most exciting trip.
But we've had men not half your age
who couldn't pass the training stage."

Grandpa stood up so erect,
said, "Young man, do I detect
a certain sense of ridicule?
Perhaps you think I am a fool,
but, my boy, let me suggest
your mob just put me to the test.
I'm old, but not decrepit yet.
Take a gamble: place your bet."

Jardine shook his greying head
quite emphatically and said,
"Pops, we know without a doubt
you'd never last the training out

and if we sent you into space,
we'd put the States right out the race.
At your great age the thing's to be
an armchair traveller. Watch TV.
Settled in your easychair,
you can go just anywhere."

Grandpa said, "Not likely, mate,
you'll change your mind and I can wait."
He set up camp outside the door.
Spreading his blanket on the floor,
he settled down to wait it out,
for of success he had no doubt.

Christmas passed, and New Year, too.
Jardine didn't know what to do.
He was becoming quite disturbed,
but Grandpa camped on, unperturbed,
playing ludo, dominoes and chess
with willing members of the press.
He shared his seeds and gumleaf tea
with Jardine's busy secretary.

Soon Grandpa's peaceful demonstration
caught the mass imagination.
People came from far and wide

to show that they were on his side.
They all marched on the NASA base,
chanting, "Let Pops go to space";
carried placards, "Don't stop Pop–
let him give it all he's got".

At last the worried president
said, "Hank, ya gotta take the gent.
Ya know this is election year.
Heck! I'll be out on my ear!"

So Grandpa took the training course,
proved himself strong as a horse,
put the young recruits to shame,
left them wond'ring why they came.
The staff at NASA begged him tell
how he stayed so fit and well.
Grandpa said, "It's gumleaf tea
that gives me my vitality.
Positive thinking does the rest.
Why not put it to the test?"

In time the ship sped past the stars
and the first man to land on Mars
was a lively geriatric gent
who knew what 'Aussie battler' meant.

The Yanks gave Pops a welcome home
that none before had ever known:
fireworks, pomp, a big brass band,
celebrations throughout the land.

At last he went on home to Gran
a happy and contented man.
She hugged him close. "I'm proud of you.
Next time would there be room for two?
I thought that Saturn might be nice,
or Venus, dear, what's your advice?"
They discussed it over parsnip soup
then went to mend the chicken coop.

And now aspiring astronauts
are taught to concentrate their thoughts.
They're fed fresh shoots and pumpkin seeds,
and assorted plants that some call weeds.
To give them their vitality
they drink a lot of gumleaf tea.

Story Worlds

Pirates in the den

Vampires in the bathroom,
pirates in the den,
burglar in the bedroom
seeking precious gem.
Climbing up the mountain
from the bottom stair.
Falling from the very top,
rushing through the air!
Indians are hiding
behind the kitchen door.
Cowboys mustn't find them
or there'll be a war.
Get beneath the table
or you will be seen!
The tablecloth's a ball gown
fit for any queen.
Soldiers in the kitchen

march to bugle call,

shot dead by the enemy,

one by one they fall.

The battle's quickly over

and there's an end to strife,

the injured are all mended,

the dead brought back to life

by the call of "Ice cream!

Anyone for cake?

Would the tired army

like to take a break?"

Digging through to China

beneath the lemon tree;

setting sail for India

across the grassy sea.

Stars of circus big top

flying on trapeze,

such amazing things

we can do with ease

up behind the garden shed

on the monkey bars.

Before it's time for dinner,

we'd best come back from Mars.

Snarling tabby tiger,

water spouting snake,

we're in dreadful danger

every step we take

through the lupin jungle

on a great safari,

hunting brontosaurus

by the rockery.

Prospecting for nuggets,

spying for the cause,

our imagination

opens up the doors

to adventure and excitement.

Who needs to travel far?

There's a world for exploration

exactly where we are.

No everyday chair

You see sitting there
A plain everyday chair.
Not I. No, I spy
With adventurer's eye
A rocket to zoom
Us out of this room
To planets and stars
Beyond Venus and Mars.

Next we take a trip
On my old sailing ship;
Defeat pirates galore
Before we put to shore
To rest for a while
On a tropical isle.

Oh no! A wild beast
Wants us for its feast.
Its jaws snap and gnash.
We escape in a flash.
My plane flies us high,
And we're safe in the sky.

When next we land
A grand marching band
Waits there to greet us
And after the fuss
We're soon on my train
Heading back home again.

Now our play's done
It's "Goodbye, everyone!"
And my chair I choose
For an end of day snooze.

Prince

Once upon a long ago
lived a prince who didn't know
he ought to ride a charger white,
rescue damsels from their plight.

Instead he travelled far and wide
with a jackass by his side;
ran from dragons and from knights,
passed his days in flying kites.

One day a princess chanced to come
upon him sleeping in the sun.
She kissed him there beside the road
and lo! he turned into a toad.

Storyteller

Storyteller, storyteller,
tell a tale or two.
Storyteller, storyteller,
tell a story, do,
of dinosaurs and monsters,
of dragons' eggs and more,
of slippery, slidey serpents
that slither through the door
and crawl upon the carpet
into my room at night
and make me call for someone
to please put on the light.

Storyteller, storyteller,
tell me tales of yore,
of myths and magic Merlin,
of ghosts and ghouls and more.

Enough to make me shiver
and pull the sheets up close,
and tingle from my head
down to my very toes.

Storyteller, storyteller,
weave your words into
a wonderful creation
that's shared with me and you.

Book World

Tell me a tale of treasure untold,
buccaneers' bounty, jewels and gold.
Spin me a yarn of a hazardous quest,
until it is ended the hero won't rest.

Share stories of dragon, damsel and knight,
princesses rescued from a grave plight;
of monsters, aliens, mystery and magic,
adventurous, exciting, funny or tragic.

Whisk me to markets jostled by crowds.
Trek me up mountains shrouded in clouds.
Spin me through space at heart-stopping speed.
Chase me through tunnels –where do they lead?

Sail me across oceans so vast and deep,
I cannot help wonder what secrets they keep.
Lead me to forests where birds nest on high –
Wind through the trees is a whispering sigh.

Such silence and splendour fills me with awe,
inspires me to whisper, "Please show me more

of far distant places where I've not yet been.
Draw open the curtains upon the next scene."

As I travel abroad without leaving home,
I'm scientist, pirate, astronaut, gnome,
crook, cop or detective solving a crime,
anyone, anywhere, freefalling in time.

Thrill me, delight me, chill me, excite me,
amaze me, intrigue me, above all invite me
to enter a world where anything goes,
created for me in wonderful prose.

Words are my passport, ideas the key
to unlock my fancy and let it roam free.
I turn the first page to open the door
into magical Book World, its realms to explore.

The everywhere chair

The upside-down, turn-around
sky-flying plane chair;
the puff-along, pull-along
steam-screaming train chair.

The float about, boat about
adventure-bound chair;
the whiz around, falling down,
get off the ground chair.

The knitting, snug-fitting,
make way for the cat chair;
the dribbled on, scribbled on,
here baby sat chair.

The climb upon, high upon
reaching for cakes chair;
the "Sit down or get down
for goodness sakes!" chair.

The cane chair, remain chair
and come back again chair;
the crawled upon, sprawled upon
no two the same chair.

The snuggled in, cuddled in
no space to spare chair;
the so deep, go to sleep,
here and there everywhere chair.

Daffodil

Daffodil, daffodil

nod your head

if you heard

what the fairy said.

Was it a whisper,

was it a yell,

was it a call

to come to the dell

where fairies flit

and goblins groan

and gnomes sit

wistful, all alone?

For none can venture,

none can roam

far from freedom,

far from home.

Knit Knack

Auntie has a knack for knitting –
Not for her just idly sitting.
She must keep her fingers busy.
Watching them makes Lizzie dizzy.
Those needles click and clack their way
Through every second of the day.

Wherever Auntie has to go
Her knitting goes along and so
She knits in buses, taxis too,
In hairdressers' or checkout queue,
While waiting for her bread to toast,
The tea to brew, potatoes roast.

When it's time to go to sleep
She counts stitches 'stead of sheep.
Fancy patterns fill her dreams,
New designs and stitching schemes.
She started out with caps and rugs
And cosy, cuddly keep-us-snugs;
Turned the toes in socks and booties
For young lads and little cuties.

One day she said, "I'm all alone,
I need a friend to share my home."
She gathered all her bits and bobs,
The scraps of yarn from other jobs,
And set about to knit a kit
That on her windowsill could sit
Among the flowers blooming there,
Or curl up on a cosy chair.

As Auntie's fingers fairly flew,
Knitting nine and purling two,
Each stitch she cast with loving care –
Wove in a wish, a special prayer.
Four purple paws, legs green and blue,
A body lean of rainbow hue,
A twirly tail of ribbon red,
Orange ears and yellow head.

Clickety clack her needles sped,
Next button eyes, a nose of thread,
And when she'd made the final stitch
in Kit she saw a whisker twitch.
Kit stretched and yawned, began to purr,
Curled up and licked its woollen fur.

For Aunt, Knit Kit was not the end.
She knew he too would need a friend,
So used her clever knitting knack
To fill her tiny seaside shack
With creatures colourful and bright
For company each day and night.
They lived together happily,
Aunt and her yarn menagerie.

A mouse in the house

"There's a mouse in our house,"
said old Farmer Fife.
"Well, a cat will fix that,"
said his good lady wife.
But the cat clawed and spat
 at the dog – how fur flew.
Fife yelled "Out!" What a shout,
that house trembled, it's true.
Next a trap it went snap
but Mouse, she ran free.
Then a man in a van
tried his luck for a fee.
Mouse hid 'neath a lid
till the danger was past.
Hunger gnawed – soon Fife snored –
Mouse broke her long fast.
Out she crept while they slept
and feasted her fill.
"It's a pest, not our guest!"
Fife vowed, "Catch her I will."
They tried brooms and loud booms,
 every potion and powder.

But Mouse she stayed, on she played,
and her gnawing grew louder.
'Twas not food but a brood
in her round little tum.
They were born in the morn
and the one had become
Nine, no less, and oh yes,
Wife and Fife were distraught.
Those lodgers, smart dodgers
just wouldn't be caught.
In a trice those fine mice
multiplied to three score
until Fife and his wife
could not take any more.
Yes, they fled, out they sped,
left their house to the mice,
who skittered and tittered
and sighed, "This is nice."

Sir Quackalot saves the day

A tale is told,
In days of old
Of a knight in shining armour.

Sir Quackalot
Of Back Farm Plot,
'Tis said he was a charmer.

Miladies swooned,
When 'er he crooned
A serenade on the stair.

So brave of heart,
He served King Art
And Gwin, his queen so fair.

One day a beast,
A dragon fierce
Awoke from its long slumber.

Its tummy growled,
Oh how it howled,
"I have an awesome hunger."

It grilled lamb chops
and killed the crops
then roasted all the horses.

Still hunger gnawed,
And loud it roared,
"I need a few more courses."

It told the king
That he must bring
A maid each day at dawning.

"And if you don't
Then live you won't!"
It singed his beard in warning.

Queen Gwin, she wailed,
"We are assailed
By an immense disaster!"

But Quackalot
Said, "I've a plot,
We'll make a maid of plaster.

"She'll break his jaw
He'll eat no more
Our maidens will be safe then."

The court agreed
And with great speed
They fetched supplies and workmen.

They worked all night
Without respite,
By morn their maid did wait

Beside lakeside,
Securely tied
As if she feared her fate.

The dragon came
With breath of flame
And roared its satisfaction.

One mighty munch,
Oh what a crunch!
That put it out of action.

A sorry sight
Without its bite,
The dragon ran away.

E'er since that time
Folks tell in rhyme
How Quackalot saved the day.

Santa's new clothes

Santa had a problem—his special suit no longer fit.
It was snug around the tummy. When he sat, his trousers split.
One bright and early morning, Mrs Santa said:
"Dear, I must tell you something that I read.
I love you roly-poly, I love you as you are,
but if you took a health test you wouldn't get a star.
It's really most important to have a healthy heart
and if you want a long life, it's not too late to start."
Santa called in at the health club—the trainer checked him out.
She said: "We'll plan a programme that'll work without a doubt."
She booked him in for workouts three times every week,
then talked about his diet and told him what to eat.
He ate lots of fruit and vegies, chose grilled instead of fried

for every single main meal, with salads on the side.
He said no to morning tea cakes and had carrot sticks instead.
Whenever offered sweet treats, he firmly shook his head.
Santa also started walking quite early in the day and soon those extra kilos began to melt away.
He said: "I feel fantastic, this year will be a breeze.
I'll deliver all those presents without the slightest wheeze.
I won't get stuck in chimneys or struggle up steep stairs,
or stop to have a rest whenever I see chairs."
Then on Christmas Eve, a problem as Santa dressed to leave.
His suit no longer fit him except for length of sleeve.
His top was loose and baggy where tight it was before,
and when he pulled his trousers up, they slid down to the floor.

He looked at Mrs Santa. "Whatever will we do?
Perhaps some safety pins? Could you sew a
seam or two?
We need a quick solution for I really ought to
go.
The children are all waiting and I can't be late,
you know."
Mrs Santa nodded and tried to hide a smile.
"Thank goodness it's late shopping. This will
only take a while."
So that's why this year Santa won't be wearing
his red suit.
He's got a brand new outfit. Mrs Santa thinks
it's cute.
It's a bright red fleecy tracksuit for warmth in
North Pole cold,
and a pair of sporty sneakers replacing boots of
old.
For his head a woolly beanie instead of pom
pom cap.
So if one Christmas evening you should glimpse
a bearded chap
who looks a lot like Santa except he's fit and
trim,
don't think that you're mistaken, for yes, you're
right, it's him!

About the author

Teena Raffa-Mulligan looks like a responsible adult. Don't be fooled—it's a disguise. The real Teena is a kid who gets a kick out of playing with words and having adventures on the page. Her publications include poems, short stories, picture books, chapter books and middle grade novels. Teena has also worked as a journalist and editor. She loves sharing her excitement about books and writing with people of all ages and encouraging them to write their own stories and poems.

Visit Teena's website at www.teenaraffamulligan.com for information about her books and writing sessions.

www.ingramcontent.com/pod-product-compliance
Lightning Source LLC
Chambersburg PA
CBHW072101290426
44110CB00014B/1769